My name is

_____

I have read this book ☐

Date

_____

LONDON, NEW YORK, MUNICH,
MELBOURNE, AND DELHI

For Dorling Kindersley
Designer Jon Hall
Managing Editor Catherine Saunders
Art Director Lisa Lanzarini
Publishing Manager Simon Beecroft
Category Publisher Alex Allan
Production Editor Siu Yin Chan
Production Controller Kate Klahn

For LucasFilm
Executive Editor Jonathan W. Rinzler
Art Director Troy Alders
Keeper of the Holocron Leland Chee
Director of Publishing Carol Roeder

First published in Great Britain in 2009 by
Dorling Kindersley Limited,
80 Strand, London, WC2R 0RL

2 4 6 8 10 9 7 5 3 1

177790 – 10/09

A CIP catalogue record for this book is
available from the British Library

ISBN: 978-1405-35339-7

Colour reproduction by Alta Image, UK
Printed and bound by TBB, Slovakia

Discover more at
www.dk.com
www.starwars.com

My name
is C-3PO.

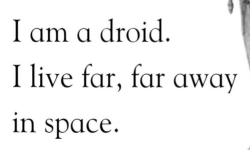

I am a droid.
I live far, far away
in space.

There are hundreds of planets in space with lots of different creatures on them. Come and explore some of the planets and meet some of my friends.

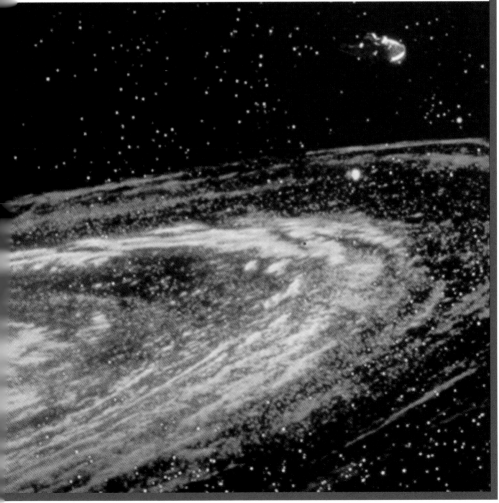

This is my friend R2-D2.
He is a droid too.

R2-D2 likes talking.
His voice sounds like
whistles and beeps, but
I can understand him.

R2-D2 is a very clever
little machine. He has all sorts
of useful tools. He can use them
to fix almost anything!

Let's take a trip to the centre of the galaxy and explore a planet named Coruscant (CORE-RUS-SANT).

It is a very important planet.

Coruscant is covered by one enormous city. Most of the buildings in that city are tall, gleaming skyscrapers.

Jedi Knights

Coruscant was home to Yoda and the rest of the Jedi Order.

Yoda

Now let's travel to a far away planet and meet Luke Skywalker.

This planet is called Tatooine
(TAT-OO-EEN). It is a
dangerous planet, covered in a
huge desert.

Luke dreams of leaving Tatooine
and having adventures.

Tatooine may be remote, but it's also home to a famous Jedi Master, Obi-Wan Kenobi.

Obi-Wan tells Luke all about being a Jedi. He also tells Luke that Luke's father was a Jedi called Anakin Skywalker.

Anakin Skywalker was once a great and powerful Jedi Knight. But Anakin turned to the dark side of the Force.

He became a Sith lord known as Darth Vader.

Darth Vader's body was damaged in a battle with Obi-Wan Kenobi. He wears a special black helmet and armour to protect it.

Darth Vader wants to rule the galaxy.

Some people want to stop him. They have joined together and are called the Rebel Alliance.

Let's journey to a floating city in the skies of the planet Bespin. This city is called Cloud City.

Visitors come to come to learn about the city's state-of-the-art mining facilities.

Lando Calrissian

The Baron Administrator of Cloud City is called Lando Calrissian (LAN-DO CAL-RIZ-E-EN). Lando is friends with a Rebel pilot called Han Solo.

Han Solo is a smuggler from the
planet Corellia (COR-ELL-E-AH).
He helps the Rebel Alliance to
defeat the Empire.

Han Solo's starship is called the *Millennium Falcon*. His co-pilot and best friend is a Wookiee called Chewbacca.

Chewbacca

Tarfful

Wookiees are tall creatures with lots of shaggy fur. Their home planet is Kashyyyk (KASH-ICK). It is a world of giant trees and shallow lakes.

Wookiees talk in a mixture of grunts and roars. They are brave and loyal creatures. Chewbacca would risk his life for his friend Han Solo.

Princess Leia is the twin sister of Luke Skywalker but she does not live on Tatooine. Princess Leia lives on a planet named Alderaan (AL-DER-AN). She is part of the Rebel Alliance.

Darth Vader destroys Alderaan with the powerful Death Star.

Darth Vader is
Princess Leia's
father too.

This is Yoda. He is a Jedi Master. He lives on a swamp planet called Dagobah (DAY-GO-BER).

Luke Skywalker visits Yoda.
Yoda trains Luke to be a Jedi.

The planet of Naboo is home to humans and Gungans.
The people live on the land. Padmé Amidala was once Queen of Naboo. She is Luke and Leia's mother.

Queen Amidala

The Gungans live
in underwater
cities. They can
walk on land too,
although some
are a bit clumsy!
Jar Jar Binks
is a Gungan.

*Jar Jar
Binks*

The forest moon of
the planet Endor is
the home of small,
furry creatures called
Ewoks. They live in the trees
and use simple tools.

The Ewoks believe that I am some sort of god and worship me. But they are less fond of my friend R2-D2!

I hope that you have enjoyed your trip to the *Star Wars* galaxy. Come back soon!

Quiz!

1. Who is Luke's father?

2. What is this droid's name?

3. Who is this?

4. Who teaches Luke to be a Jedi?

Answers: 1. Anakin Skywalker, 2. C-3PO, 3. Princess Leia, 4. Yoda